T0304563

Book design: Sandra Rosales
Cover image: Na Forest Lim
Published: Gold Line Press
http://goldlinepress.com
Gold Line titles are distributed by Small Press Distributions
This title is also available for purchase directly from the publisher
www.spdbooks.org: 800.869.7553

Library of Congress Cataloging-in-Publication Data
Flower Boi
Library of Congress Control Number 2022947905
Marshall, Mars
ISBN 978-1-938900-47-1

FLOWER
BOI

MARS MARSHALL

GOLD LINE PRESS

CONTENTS

I.

II.

I

The BOI's Failed Crown

what do I make with this mess of flowers
tansy & verbena make my mouth declare war
& prayer in one breath make my body a maze
of thorns intimacy spoiled by a lover's casual
kiss softness a memory ground into dust
my skin cold soaked with longing Black & then
what night holds is a false promise, hardened spine
& if not for the I then what else keeps the BOI whole?
the I licks Their lips & says I'm a good thing
feels for the roof of Their mouth & thinks rigid
wanting teeth, how space can be both void and
full is a trick only the BOI knows well the I is a
hymnal unworthy of Their mother's tongue
what is the BOI if not sometimes an apology?

the BOI sometimes an apology is a wingless
bird stretching before the sun blinks a new day
into existence, BOI incapable of flight is pulled
closely into the body of a stranger, the I knows
the chicanery of night – how it cradles the moon
knowing it will always slip away, to be desired
(even temporarily) is enough to feed the I's ego
to open the BOI's mouth wide & cram Their
jaws with everything they will one day lose
sense of self, what it feels like to be touched –
how to soften, the liberty to pop & twist &
shake & move underneath flashing lights, what
it's like to be called home or called by name
a jolt causing the I to return to Their body

the I returns to Their body see the BOI
cradling an indigo child – small fingers
wrapped around the I a tiny squeeze –
BOI searches the infant's face for memory
asks the I *who this body belongs to, what
is a name* the indigo child yawns, becomes
ghost-like – a dream sequence the I was once
a parade of daffodils swaying in the sun's
crooked mouth I once a glimmer in their
mother's wheat eyes – the son she always
wanted swaddled in pink garments adorned
in glitter, accidental girl dressed in ruffles
the I wilts in the grip of Their mother's
religion call the I unholy or call the BOI whole

                    Call the BOI whole, the I holy
                    God said *let there be light &* then
                    there was light cascading down the
                    I BOI drenched in rain – a good
                    watering fit for a peculiar bloom
                    the Black BOI is not an anomaly
                    is instead a whisper exchanged
                    among bodies sitting on a wooden
                    pew sweet saints sweet stain ruining
                    the choir robes the I sings & no-
                    one applauds Pastor says BOI take flight
                    so the I searches for the heaven all BOIs
                    belong to where a cacophony of organ
                    chords praise the I praise the BOI – Their body

I Want to Be a
Happy BOI

Can I fit into your arms BOI and tell you of the time
a wolf crawled into my body, its sharp eyes
becoming mine, the scowl mistaken for a
kind smile, the lonely wander in winter woods mine.

The wolf's full   moon   mouth   begged
to taste January's stillness, its sharp bite. I know
the space between the wolf's fullness and my own.

BOI, you are whole and fitting to yourself & I've asked
who this body belongs to, its bleeding wants, weighty limbs
dark skin, its stranger mouth.

ETYMOLOGY

BOY
noun, often attributive | 'bȯi'

1.   a: male child from birth to adulthood

My father was once hit by a car
while on his way to visit a girl on the West Side
of Detroit.

His teenage hormones guiding him into traffic
body laying full on blacktopped streets and sure
he was okay but named a foolish boy.

Foolish boy met my mother
while they were bubble gum smack young.
My mother noting all the girls foolishly

batting their eyes at my father. I have no
reference for how they became a couple
just that they became pregnant with me

and soon after but before I came a marriage
would mark their union by God in a
church knowing some of his secrets.

My father, foolish man
with wandering hands always found another
body to mark as home.

My grandfather apologized
to my mother, for every moment my father
fell short of being a good man.

On summer nights, he'd sit on the porch
with her and say *I'm sorry, daughter*
I don't know what's wrong with my boy.

b: son

When our mothers no longer call us home
the night swallows our bodies into a rhythm
endless, our movements strobing as the disco

ball hangs with obligation, my body
a shadow casts on the wall in obligation
knowing that BOIs don't move, stand

in a pair of Girbaud or Sean John jeans with
braids tucked neatly under the 59Fifty as T,
an older stud, ushers us into a night we're sure

to forget. Dark stank clinging to my spine,
DJ begs us to forget our first names, I drink
and forget the way it feels when a mother no

longer calls you hers or when a mother forgets
you have her first name, this ritual of giving to
the night sky with prayer tucked underneath

my tongue, I beg to find my father here – savior
who calls me his Son, a boy who smiles the same
way he did when he was young.

Once I tried on my father's clothes found his gun
in the closet and thought *this is what makes a man*
so I tried on the gun, pulled and pulled until my

face became metal, my mouth the hollow home
of a bullet each time a woman said I was
worthy of love then said *son, you trippin'*

BOI
noun, often attributive | 'bȯi'

2.   a: term coined to describe masculine presenting queer
       Black folk

       When used referring to my body, I origami
       crane, fold in the intricate shape
       of masculinity – see my delicate angles

       lines drawn perfect, the folding is a narrative
       belonging to BOIs like me, who craft themselves
       a worthy fit to hold a woman the way boys do

       with a gentleness incapable of breaking,
       until the same woman laughs at soft
       parts rendering BOIs worthy of a joke.

My mother says she didn't raise a son
as her back hand makes any argument
fall down my throat.

FLOWER BOI

Back in the day –
you snapped the heads of dandelions
from their bodies, watched them
swim in a jar of water and gifted
them to your mother.
You were the beautiful thing,
who, before being called to dinner,
dug your hands deep
into the yard's soft belly
pulled the writhing worm and too
snapped its head before burying it
into the same ground you disturbed.
You snapped the chicken
wings apart before being told to say grace first.

What can be said of your own breaking?
Lover reaching into night bloom black
blue; your own neck still against
a lover's cruel palm, your open mouth
sound caught in the esophagus. Day broke
same as you, a ruby morning.

The BOI Rushes To

feat. Frank Ocean

Saturdays involved making our entrances into life outside / We've been in this room too long / Recreation is keeping us self-contained and aware / Of each other's form

Her hair scattered across my bathroom, bedroom floors
Door the shape of her frame, voice echoing in my blood chambers

A body not yet full is easily consumed A body not yet full
is a question Good reason for leaving I am to blame

She more fleeting than I'd like her to be brief history
we loved once and that became a fog filled night loud silence

Once we asked *what if*, question becoming spell sweet ghost
haunting the halls of my lonely, whispering of all I deserve

while naming me unworthy beast

*

Son who leave / The son who leaves

A weighted sky calls my mother to prayer /her/ near *God* listening
amongst the noise my body covered in Christian magic saved despite –

I, a BOI once her pink miracle given /her/ name & wishing well
of a tongue, I pray to be poured into the body she didn't choose for me
sweet Black son hiding in the shadow of

himself Once – a scripture tumbled from my soft lips & I awoke the next
morning with my father's face wide grin /his/ boyish charm, the woman
asleep next to me nothing like my mother /

her/ hardened spine faithfulness, instead a woman calls me hers & forgets
to add *temporarily* I stay listen closely to the whistling pines find
my mother in a field weeping among

them & when I bring /her/ face close to mine she says *come home
come home* though I never left

*

And rewind it back one more / The tape stopped before I was back alone

If I had the crown of a peacock
all the ill-intentioned loves
the I in my BOI loves so badly

I could ward off every predator
gather at the front door
sometimes I mean I love myself

I love just as my mother taught me
with the faith of a mustard seed I
mean I trusted the metaphor, that
faith and prayer could yield a vast
love, a last love —all my BOIshness
cradled in her midnight sky eyes —

*

LYCANTHROPY

In my dreams I was a boy some past life sends his ghost when
I am in a deep slumber sometimes, he is a wolf not one that howls at the moon,
but one that sinks his teeth into the neck of a woman,

sends her howling instead of himself, & he visits her when
he is tired & sometimes he's alone & wanders too wild for a place to call home
understands the brevity of a moment

> *lost out*
> > *beat up*
> > > *dancin'*

> > > *down there*

in a dream, I am at the altar
donning lipstick, a French
manicure, hair wound in
curls, body, draped in my mother's vows

> the wolf stands at the altar
> absent of a smile a tear falls
> from his left eye

the falsehood of being his wife
sends me howling & at midnight

the moon feels hidden well
& I can be found 'round there

dancin' outside of my body

twilight comes & the wolf comes for me throws his head back pries
my ribs open says I come from him

& when I ask him for a name
he gives me my name

shows his teeth & it is not a threat
& the wolf howls

if ya mama knew
how you turned out
you too wild
you too wild

in a dream I am in bed with a strange woman & the boy doesn't sleep
tonight, the wolf wanders the yard, the falsehood of my body held
in the arms of a woman who loves me in fragments

I tell her she found me *lost & beat u*p
& she claims to know I was *warm flesh*

unseasoned & she sleeps here without

                    knowing who I've become

Abecedarian on Dysphoria

anytime a wolf howls, the moon shakes
becomes a dead falcon in the sky or my father

calls me the son he's always wanted, once
day broke into a million shards of glass – fell on

Earth; sea made of wolves' teeth, blood-bathed my
familiar curves into an unfit body full

grown inside a stranger – peel her skin from myself
howl at the dawnless sky and cover each limb in fur

imagine who we'd be if our first breath was ours to take
joined in song with our mothers' brokenness

kindred in the legacy of loneliness thickening
linger here in the vastness of a night's long kiss

mend the bruise from needle piercing the flesh
noisy heart hum – bird flutter, pour obsidian

over my head and watch me disappear
pacify the gnawing ache and let me wake a perfect BOI

quiet my trembling limbs and say *I am enough*
remember a lover's night calling me into my body

silence, as her finger caresses the open wound
takes me into herself and calls me worthy

ugly twisted day, my crooked mouth on display
view the BOI who turned wolf at the sight of the moon

weep as the lover twists my fur into tiny knots
xerox this image and make a list of strange things

yellow yesterday or girl an apparition dancing in shadow
zero in on my features, dare me monstrous call me gorgeous

Cartography

I try to make a map of my body
See which roads lead me to drink from
a river made by my hands.

Which veins bend toward a rising sun?
What valley kneels to the day setting?

I am deliberate in my making.

Run my hands over the surface
of my flesh to raise a softer BOI
to take stock of mountains

claiming home to Them, too.
I am watercolor and ink on gesso,

vibrant and my own.

I peer into reflective glass
and draw the lines of me crooked.
Find beauty in what is also distorted.

I try to make a map
to never forget myself

in the early morning when my body
says no good no good no --
I look across the terrain, to remind myself

of all this beauty.

My Mother Asks If I Plan on Changing My Name

imagine a thing that's yours until it isn't:
the kitchen sink full of chipped plates
a small cut along the width of your thumb
two women's suits
in your bedroom closet
a half-eaten mango rotting in the fridge
long hair clogging the tub's drain
your father's sentiment to name
you after two women
in his life though he
couldn't care for either of them   & so
you carry a name with confused pride, google yourself &
find the gaggle of white women who share your name
you're taken back to a moment when a waiter at the Mediterranean
restaurant returns your debit card then asks
how you got your name before spending several
minutes telling you what it means
Showerer of blessings Showerer of blessings
you remember the playground filled
with nasally children who said you have an old person's name
and even as you call yourself, your tongue is thick
with cottage cheese, falls slack when in your
own mouth acknowledge its drawl
how it sounds as if it belongs to a country singer
or to a brand of hand-stitched cardigans sold
at Sears

or your mother
how her mother
gave it to her first
& now she looks at you
your new mustache
cheeks faint with hair
& sees a daughter once was
remembers you both
share the same name
& of course you wish
you could give it back
but your father is already
dead.

Self Portrait as a BOI Born into Wealth

My silver spoon melted into fronts   drip

I never question my worth
pull Versace from the closet & turn   my own head
dress because I am the occasion

buy the Swarovski Silver Bullet Nike Air
Max 97's simply because I can

I'm the bullet lodged in my own teeth   smile b****

I watch the stock market for entertainment
collect rare bottles of whiskey as trophies

flash my wrist in the zoom camera because
who doesn't want to see me shine

I call my mother just to say I'm alive and listen
to none of what she has to say I visit my father's grave to take selfies

here lays the man who gave me much

order me filet mignon and lobster tail over a creamy bed of polenta
make my bed and watch me f* it up

I lament over breakfast
break into a sun ignored

tell you polish my nails and call me gorgeous   why?
'cause I demand it

I'm the solar eclipse
a rarity in your textbooks

I splurged on college just because
scroll Twitter to feel relatable

I'm simply   devastating
my girlfriend(s) say so

in the city I buy a whole block   to be remembered
ain't no BOI better

put diamonds on my birthday cake   & make a wish

FRANK SPEAKS TO FLOWER BOI
with selected lyrics from the album Endless

We've been here before, our backs to the stars as we whisper small prayers
to our moons. We are lonely boys, half bloomed.
Boys with mothers who worry. Boys who tuck want in the folds of our bodies
and pretend it cannot be found.

I knew a bully boy who stood on the greenest grass and begged
to become a garden. His balled fist pounding Earth. Knuckles raised
with mud caked to them. All that boy wanted was someone to love him,
to twirl the ends of his braids and kiss his forehead.

We've been there too, wrote the ballads, signed our loneliness over
to whoever wanted a good cry. There's something you need,
someone out there who is not a clock.
I'm reminding myself of this too.

Feelings come, feelings go and I guess you can't blame the ones
you choose. Those starlit girls who smile in the distance,
ones you've reached for in the night, their bodies apparition.
What stays and what- what's gone and what's here still?

BOI softened, with each passing love. I say this to you
because I also need to be reminded of it. Forever will be much closer
than it is now to your Earth dipped skin. Your heart flutter hum.
You anxious BOI, tired of waiting for love to come.

You, who turn your palms upward,
gaze at the sky, proclaim *I leave myself at
the mercy of you*, and know that God chuckles.

II

On Pleasure

In the garden, sun flowers lean their heads
long toward the golden mouth of summer sun.
They crowd the yard with chatter of BOIs who turn
soft when night's hand, palms the sacred plump.
Delicate just as we are, the sun flowers say, the nectar sweet too,
my my—how silence catches their throats when
asked if we can have our fill; how hard disintegrates
when you call a song to rise from Their soft bellies.
(The sun flowers call their masc—beauties fool's gold.)
Teach me pleasure without its gendered performance
and let a BOI be taken by the moon if They so desire.
Offer no proof for why They are worthy of the rain's
gentle blessing.

Responding to the Question:
"Do you see yourself?"

A lover's mouth chews *you are so good so good such a good lover*
as we lay in the narrow space of night – this sliver of good
sliding between our fingers the dampness of our skin a temporary
stay *no you are you are* tumbles from my begging throat an act
of deflection *I am not good no good no good of a lover*

And what proof does *seeing* offer if there is only ever leaving
if there is only ever the slow chokehold of loneliness proving
delicate hands capable of – **{gasp}** – the lover's small fingers wrapped
around my throat – here I am almost worthy of being seen

I can't say I have seen myself
whole blooming in an empty field
but the empty field – the vacant space
of my body, how I am taken into the mouth a woman
who will take what she needs and leave always

Yes – I know, there's more to seeing myself
than how I call a lover into me – & when she
marks me a good thing I search for a small
place – hang my wants on morning's crooked teeth

No

I saw myself once – a hungry wolf taking a woman
into my wide mouth feast of longing feast of invisible
the first lesson on being seen – be gift giver silence
mistaken for kindness, soft peach flesh be still
be anything but taken be easily forgotten
hardly seen

I've twisted my tongue into new tongues.
Spoke a language with no name.

There is truth I seek in my own pleasure
my body writhing under the palms of another.

I give my flesh over to what dampens the sky
with rain. Shed until I grow a new skin.

When she calls me, I break open as cumulonimbus.
A vertical tower full and dark.

I pour until there is nothing left, glint
in the moon's bite.

I was bred to be taken into the mouth
of a woman who curses her own tongue.

She splits my spine and a snake
fuses the rupture.

We Were Strangers

until the DJ called us into each other, your damp face beautiful
we sway and pelvic press on the dancefloor here a dimly lit club

with other bodies drunk on delight their unknowing faces fade
into a different night, you say *wanna get out of here* and I follow

into a night where winter quiets and the moon full belly laughs

and I forget my own name as you say it, all my desires tumbling into
each other – we fuck and it's not by accident, I hold you and understand

the measure of a body only good enough to give and give and give –
I forget my own name and you say it as you leave out of the front door

Again, the BOI falls for a woman with kind eyes a warming touch
night calls and the BOI answers.

ODE TO THE STUD [1]

A gaggle of birds flock to the street under the arc
of a red oak in summer's hot breath.
Look, at how they gather, their wings pulled back
chests poked out. Song never escapes their taut
beaks. I wonder, what mutes their melody?
How their colors warn an enemy or call a lover
home. And I wonder too, if they find becoming
a matter of instinct or a matter of undoing?

On Saturday nights, my BOIs and I perch along
the wall of a tiny nightclub on the Eastside
sweat and fried chicken wafting in the air.
We shed our skins so often, many times in the car
as Wayne blares through the speakers.
Because Steph's mom found her strap in the closet
and beat her the color of a roadside flare we all swore
to never leave home the way our mothers
didn't intend for us; with the 59 Fifty
atop our fresh braids or our jeans just below
the start of our ass.

---

[1] **Stud** – term used to describe black masculine presenting women. Coined from black
lesbian communities to separate from the term 'butch'

Club Pink on Saturday Night
Detroit, MI - 2008

Pink alludes to softness says soften says cotton candy flip wrist & watch
the femme spin flip hair back look back at it & slay all us Stud so hard
clench jaw & smile sometimes shot girl carries the rainbow in a shooter
maybe tequila maybe vodka drink to being to the bass's heavy hand against
your chest drink to the night & its longing you are not one for being seen
though being here is to be seen work this lesbian scene course through
desire like everyone else Pink & pulsing she licks her lips says come come
come & everything quiets it's midnight & you are now part of her show
the slow grind against your pelvis sway with her everyone is watching wipe
the sweat from your brow ignore the throb in you think pink & bite your
bottom lip

ODE TO THE STUD[1]

I snapped the head of a Venus flytrap
and became monstropolous. Buried
its tongue treasure in the pockets
of my cheeks and curled against
a body, same as my own. The tips
of her fingers lingered along my spine.
I palmed her braids, praised her softest
parts. The moon flashed its flashy teeth
while we took the quiet moment before
night reaches for the tiny pleasure we can
not name. Sweet sweet taboo to cause
the arch in her BOI back. To whisper
you could be mine someday and mean
how lovely to dismiss the fem's snarled
dismay of two hard bodies twisted in the
shadows. To gently wipe the sweat from
her arched brow. To hold her close the way
two Studs do after a win on hardwood.
She will say what she wants by morning.
She will forget my name.

[1] **Stud** –As a rule, Studs do not date other Studs.

Call Them by Their name

○

       tell Them the story,
       about a bird that flew into
       your window, how its dizzy
       head smacked into the glass,
       startled you so bad
       you spilled coffee on your kitchen
       floor. watch the awe and shock splay
       across Their face, consider the softness
       in Their eyes. tell Them the bird
       was okay, that you know this because you
       ran downstairs to check on the fleeting creature,
       how you scooped it up in a blanket, whispered
       a spell, and watched it take flight again.

○ ○

       hold Them the night a full moon shines
       its teeth and know Their body's ache
       to shine in the night sky without validation.
       acknowledge the lantern of you, a brilliant
       woman refusing to hush their wants. They
       fit against your body gentleness singing
       a lullaby so perfect They sleep
       instead of scream.

O O O

Call Them by Their name.

O O O O

when Their body blooms a beautiful invasive
species. Do not wash Them off or ask Them to
unpack the haunting reminder, of what keeps
Them tucked into shame.
Whisper a good spell when twilight
wakes you with wonder of who They are,
and watch them take flight.

Ode to Feeding My Homies

When the belly is full & the mouth more than satisfied
I glow in the silence.

Relish in how a good meal brings about celebration
for all we have together.

To hold each other & say this too is good & we nourish
ourselves with laugher or an honest conversation

over a hot bowl of stew poured neatly atop a bed of rice.

We were once too broke to have such lavish meals
suggested by the NYTimes or Bon Appetit.

Took all the change we had in our jars to conjure up
spaghetti or dressed up ramen

Sweating over the stove or in summer heat
watching the lit coals smoke the meat done

we cackle often and sometimes cry too.
Break bread and allow a sweet hush to fall over the room.

How holy it is, to grab the light of us and say, friend
I want to ensure you are full.

To take all this gratitude I have for you and knead the dough
massage the kale & mix a vinaigrette to please the gods.

Imagine Being Loved by Another BOI

with such tenderness even the peonies
stick around longer than intended to
watch the swell of sweetness bloom
across your brown faces and who can
deny the pleasure of witnessing two
BOIs cackle under the cracking weight
of the sun in all its seasons holding each
other delicate like the fuzzy stem of sun
flowers beautiful in the absence of despair
an honest longing filled as they look into
each other as if the world has simply faded
away and when they call their names it's as
if the name always belonged in their mouths
ever flowing in the delight in saying *i choose
you i choose you again and again* in summer's
tender heat & as the trees shed to fall asleep &
as the snow slow dances & to wake again again
when the crocuses peak their heads from under
ground to bring a succulent fruit to their lips
& say *for you my love, for you*

How To Cube A Mango

cradle the fruit/ in your palm/over a bowl/using a peeler/ strip half/
of the mango/ take a knife/ slice tender yellow lengthwise ||||||| against
the seed/ sweet juice/ runs the length/ of your fingers/ taste/_____ /
take the knife/ cut tender yellow crosswise/once complete/ run the knife/ under/
freshly cut tender yellow/ along the seed/watch the pieces/_____ / fall/ along
the tips of/ or/ between/your fingers //

turn and repeat

                                        / until /tender/
                                        yellow falls

                                        clean/

                                    suck what remains/ until the
                        seed/ is bare

            until the seed is bare

I find myself/breast in the hands/ of a lover, I tell them/using a knife,
strip/the front half of my body/the first layer/beyond blemished/ black
skin glistens/let them praise/what runs the length/of their fingers,
allow/their temptations to taste/ hand them the knife/ask them
to cut lengthwise/tender plump protruding flesh/ tell them to run
the knife/along the breastplate, clean/
watch the pieces/

        fall/

along the tips of/

      or between/

           their fingers/

my body sculpted in the palms of their hands

Notes and Acknowledgments

The definitions in "ETYMOLOGY" are pulled from Merriam-Webster dictionary with the final definition pulled from Michigan State University's LGBTQIA+ Glossary.

The epigraphs in "The BOI Rushes To" is pulled from Frank Ocean's infamous album entitled Endless, on which the track "Rushes To" appears.

Although Kanye West is no longer in right relationship with us... LYCANTHROPY uses lyrics found in his song entitled "Wolves," which are marked using italics.

Background text in "On Pleasure" is pulled from the brief refrain in Frank Ocean's song entitled "God Speed."

"FRANK SPEAKS TO THE BOI" uses selected lyrics from Frank Ocean's album *Endless*. The following lyrics are used: We've been here before ("Rushes"), Take the bully on the greenest grasses ("Alabama"), Feelings come, feelings go ("Comme des Garçons"), There's something you need someone out there ("In Here Somewhere"), Guess you can't blame the ones you choose ("Slide on Me"), What stays and what-what's gone and what's here still ("Rushes To")

Much gratitude to the publications featuring poems that appear in this manuscript.

"I want to be a happy BOI" first appeared in *Gertrude Press*, Issue 30.

"Etymology" previously entitled "BOY" first appeared in *Cosmonauts Avenue*.

"The BOI Rushes To" first appeared in *Michigan Quarterly Review*: Mixtape, Issue 6.

"Abecedarian on Dysphoria," "FLOWER BOI," "FRANK SPEAKS TO FLOWER BOI, and "ODE TO THE STUD" first appeared in *Obsidian: Literature & Arts in the African Diaspora*, Volume 47.

"Responding to the Question: 'Do you see yourself?'", "Call Them by Their Name", and "LYCANTHROPY" first appeared in Emerge: *2019 Lambda Fellows Anthology*.

"Club Pink on Saturday Night" first appeared in *Knights Library Magazine*.

"How to Cube Mango" and " The BOI's Failed Crown" first appeared in *Foglifter Journal*: Volume 5, Issue 2.

"The BOI's Failed Crown" also appeared in *Michigan Quarterly Review Online's Special Issue: Why We Write*.

For my dearest friends and comrades whom the sun shines for: Kristle Marshall, Brittany Rogers, Ajanaé Dawkins, Nandi Comer, Tommye Blount, Inam Kang, Tariq Luthun, Molly Raynor, Franny Choi, Morgan Willis, Corina Fadel, Vanessa Reynolds, LaShaun Phoenix Moore, Imani

Nichele, Bakpak Durden, ill weaver, Sophiyah E, Charlotte Abotsi, Laurel Chen, Duji Tahat, Gordon Palmer, Amina Mans, Devin Samuels, Tawana Petty, and many blessings to the ones who raised me.

MARS is a writer and cultural organizer born and raised in Detroit. Their work has been published in Obsidian Literature & Arts for the African Diaspora, Michigan Quarterly Review: The Mixtape, Foglifter Journal, Gertrude Press, and elsewhere. MARS is a 2021 Kresge Literary Arts Fellow in Poetry and a 2019 Lambda Literary Art Emerging Writers Fellow in Poetry.